P9-DOC-936

Meditations from

A
SIMPLE
PATH

MOTHER TERESA

Meditations from

A SIMPLE PATH

Excerpted from *A Simple Path*
Compiled by Lucinda Vardey

Ballantine Books • *New York*

ISBN: 0-345-40699-0

Text design by Holly Johnson
Manufactured in the Unites States of America

First edition: March 1996
10   9   8   7   6   5   4   3   2   1

INTRODUCTION

☙

I have had the great fortune to meet Mother Teresa on several occasions. Each time, I was struck by her deep love for God and overwhelming sense of peace. The desire to experience this peace is, in fact, what draws so many of us to her. Mother Teresa herself would respond, if asked, that it is not she who is the source of this peace, but God. With this book, all of us are welcome to seek the path to peace which she has followed in the hope that we may find the same.

In an age of misplaced priorities, we may need to be reminded of the importance of faith in God and the joy to be received from experiencing this faith. It is a simple message, yet one many of us do not readily see. Too often, faith suffers under the burdens of the modern world. Yet, it is faith that gives each of us the strength to overcome our difficulties because God's love is enduring. We learn through faith that we are not facing our struggles alone.

For almost fifty years, Mother Teresa has dedicated her life to serving the poorest of the poor. She has witnessed, in the slums of Calcutta, how God's love transforms lives. Where many others might see only suffering, Mother Teresa sees dignity. Indeed, it is the poorest, who are not consumed with worldly matters, who are most free to seek God's peace.

Each of us has the opportunity to share in this peace. For many accustomed to a fast-paced world filled with anxiety, this may seem difficult at first, but this book offers us a guide. The path to faith begins with silent contemplation and prayer. Prayer frees us from worldly concerns and reminds us of God's constant presence in our lives. Once we are able to accept God's love through prayer, we will be able to share this love with others through service.

Not all of us are called to serve in the particular way that Mother Teresa and the Missionaries of Charity serve, but we are called to serve others in everyday life. It is not how much we do that is important; rather, it is the love with which our actions are performed that is most important. The smallest action, done with love, will lead us toward peace.

The beauty of the messages in this simple volume is that they speak not only to Catholics but to people of all faiths. They are simple truths that transcend all boundaries of race, culture, and religion.

They offer all of us a guide on the path to peace. As you read these words, I encourage you to open your hearts to God in prayer and to welcome His peace.

Anthony Cardinal Bevilacqua
Archbishop of Philadelphia

February 8, 1996

THE SIMPLE PATH

The fruit of silence is
PRAYER.
The fruit of prayer is
FAITH.
The fruit of faith is
LOVE.
The fruit of love is
SERVICE.
The fruit of service is
PEACE.

THE
FRUIT
OF
SILENCE
IS
PRAYER

I always begin my prayer in silence, for it is in the silence of the heart that God speaks. God is the friend of silence—we need to listen to God because it's not what we say but what He says to us and through us that matters. Prayer feeds the soul—as blood is to the body, prayer is to the soul—and it brings you closer to God. It also gives you a clean and pure heart. A clean heart can see God, can speak to God, and can see the love of God in others.

If you are searching for God and do not know where to begin, learn to pray and take the trouble to pray every day. You can pray anytime, anywhere. You can pray at work—work doesn't have to stop prayer and prayer doesn't have to stop work. Tell Him everything, talk to Him. He is our father, He is father to us all whatever religion we are. We are all created by God, we are his children. We have to put our trust in Him and love Him, believe in Him, work for Him. And if we pray, we will get all the answers we need.

Without prayer I could not work for even half an hour. I get my strength from God through prayer.

Start and end the day with prayer. Come to God as a child. If you find it hard to pray you can say, "Come Holy Spirit, guide me, protect me, clear out my mind so that I can pray." When you pray, give thanks to God for all His gifts because everything is His and a gift from Him. Your soul is a gift of God. If you are Christian, you can say the Lord's Prayer; if Catholic, the Our Father, the Hail Mary, the Rosary, the Creed—all common prayers. If you or your family have your own devotions, then pray according to them.

Every night before you go to bed you must make an examination of conscience (because you don't know if you will be alive in the morning!). Whatever is troubling you, or whatever wrong you may have done, you need to repair it. Remember that God is merciful, He is the merciful father to us all. We are His children and He will forgive and forget if we remember to do so.

MAKE
YOUR
FAMILY
A
FAMILY
OF
LOVE

Prayer is needed for children and in families. Love begins at home and that is why it is important to pray together. If you pray together you will stay together and love each other as God loves each one of you.

A PRAYER TO THE
HOLY FAMILY

Heavenly Father, You have given us a model of life in the Holy Family of Nazareth. Help us, O loving Father, to make our family another Nazareth where love, peace, and joy reign.

May it be deeply contemplative, intensely Eucharistic, and vibrant with joy.

Help us to stay together in joy and sorrow through family prayer.

Teach us to see Jesus in the members of our family, especially in His distressing disguises.

May the Eucharistic Heart of Jesus make our hearts meek and humble like His and help us to carry out our family duties in a holy way.

May we love one another as God loves each one of us more and more each day, and forgive each other's faults as You forgive our sins.

Help us, O loving Father, to take whatever You give and to give whatever You take with a big smile.

Immaculate Heart of Mary, cause of our joy, pray for us.

Saint Joseph pray for us.

Holy Guardian Angels be always with us, guide and protect us.

Amen.

People ask me what advice I have for a married couple struggling in their relationship. I always answer "Pray and forgive"; and to young people who come from violent homes, "Pray and forgive"; and to the single mother with no family support, "Pray and forgive." You can say, "My Lord, I love You. My God, I am sorry. My God, I believe in You. My God, I trust You. Help us to love one another as You love us."

GOD

IS

A

FRIEND

OF

SILENCE

∾

We all need time for silence, to re-flect and to pray.

God is everywhere and in everything and we are all His children. When we gather in His name this gives us strength.

PRAY
EVERY
DAY

Try to feel the need for prayer often during the day and take the trouble to pray. Prayer makes the heart large enough until it can contain God's gift of Himself. Ask and seek, and your heart will grow big enough to receive Him and keep Him as your own.

L et us all become a true and fruitful branch on the vine Jesus, by accepting Him in our lives as it pleases Him to come:

> as the Truth—to be told;
> as the Life—to be lived;
> as the Light—to be lighted;
> as the Love—to be loved;
> as the Way—to be walked;
> as the Joy—to be given;
> as the Peace—to be spread;
> as the Sacrifice—to be offered,

in our families and within our neighborhood.

The prayers on pages 24–28 are taken from the Missionaries of Charity prayerbook.

O God, we believe You are here. We adore and love You with our whole heart and soul because You are most worthy of all our love.

We desire to love You as the Blessed do in Heaven.

We adore all the designs of Your divine Providence, resigning ourselves entirely to Your Will.

We also love our neighbor for Your sake as we love ourselves.

We sincerely forgive all who have injured us, and ask pardon of all whom we have injured.

Dear Jesus, help us to spread Your fragrance everywhere we go.

Flood our souls with Your spirit and
life.
Penetrate and possess our whole being, so
utterly,
That our lives may only be a radiance of
Yours.
Shine through us, and be so in us,
That every soul we come in contact with
may feel Your presence in our soul.
Let them look up and see no longer us,
but only Jesus!
Stay with us, and then we shall begin to
shine as You shine;
So to shine as to be a light to others.
The light O Jesus will be all from You,
none of it will be ours;

It will be You, shining on others through
us.

Let us thus praise You in the way You
love best by shining on those around
us.

Let us preach You without preaching, not
by words but by our example,

By the catching force, the sympathetic
influence of what we do,

The evident fullness of the love our
hearts bear to You.

Amen.

Deliver me, O Jesus,
From the desire of being loved,
From the desire of being extolled,
From the desire of being honored,
From the desire of being praised,
From the desire of being preferred,
From the desire of being consulted,
From the desire of being approved,
From the desire of being popular,
From the fear of being humiliated,
From the fear of being despised,
From the fear of suffering rebukes,
From the fear of being calumniated,
From the fear of being forgotten,
From the fear of being wronged,
From the fear of being ridiculed,
From the fear of being suspected.

THE
FRUIT
OF
PRAYER
IS
FAITH

God is everywhere and in everything and without Him we cannot exist.

There are so many religions and each one has its different ways of following God. I follow Christ:

> Jesus is my God,
> Jesus is my Spouse,
> Jesus is my Life,
> Jesus is my only Love,
> Jesus is my All in All,
> Jesus is my Everything.

Because of this I am never afraid.

So take whatever He gives and give whatever He takes with a big smile. Accept the gifts of God and be deeply grateful. If He has given you great wealth, make use of it, try to share it with others, with those who don't have anything. Always share with others.

We are all capable of good and evil. We are not born bad: everybody has something good inside. Some hide it, some neglect it, but it is there. God created us to love and to be loved, so it is our test from God to choose one path or the other.

We have to avoid any kind of temptation that will destroy us. We gain the strength to overcome this from prayer, because if we are close to God we spread joy and love to everybody around us.

Christ's love is always stronger than the evil in the world, so we need to love and to be loved: it's as simple as that.

EACH

LIFE

IS

PRECIOUS

TO

GOD

I see God in the eyes of every child . . . Every life is precious to God, whatever the circumstances.

There is only one God and He is God to all; therefore it is important that everyone is seen as equal before God. I've always said we should help a Hindu become a better Hindu, a Muslim become a better Muslim, a Catholic become a better Catholic.

To God, everything is simple—God's love for us is greater than all the conflicts, which will pass.

FAITH

IS

A

GIFT

OF

GOD

It is God's wish that we grow in our faith.

It is important to gain self-knowledge as part of spiritual growth—to know yourself and believe in yourself means you can know and believe in God. Knowledge of yourself produces humility, and knowledge of God produces love.

THE TREE OF
SELF-DEFEAT

In the branches: Emptiness
                    Alienation   Apathy
                    Interpersonal Conflicts
                    Crime   Dependency
                    Alcoholism
                    Drug Addiction
In the roots: Fear   Insecurity
                    Resentment   Jealousy
                    Mistrust   Hostility
                    Guilt   Self-Pity

THE TREE OF
SELF-REALIZATION

In the branches: Purposefulness

Health   Joy

Self-Motivation

Contentment

Acceptance

Fulfillment   Creativity

In the roots: Charity   Friendship

Forgiveness   Love

Gratitude   Kindness

Warmth   Trust

I

AM

ON MY

WAY

TO

HEAVEN

From a sign on the morgue of the
home for the dying and destitute,
Calcutta.

All things are decided by God. He decides when we live and when we die. We have to put our faith in Him and do the work that He has called us to do right up to when we die.

Anyone is capable of going to Heaven. Heaven is our home. Dying is not the end, it is just the beginning. Death is a continuation of life. This is the meaning of eternal life; it is where our soul goes to God, to be in the presence of God, to see God, to speak to God, to continue loving Him with greater love. We only surrender our body in death—our heart and our soul live forever.

Yesterday is gone and tomorrow has not yet come; we must live each day as if it were our last so that when God calls us we are ready, and prepared, to die with a clean heart.

❧

THE
FRUIT
OF
FAITH
IS
LOVE

❧

There are many in the world who are dying for a piece of bread but there are many more dying for a little love. There's a hunger for love, as there is a hunger for God.

When you know how much God is in love with you then you can only live your life radiating that love.

The following prayer is the prayer every Missionary of Charity says before leaving for his or her Apostolate. It is also used as the Physician's Prayer in Shishu Bhavan, the children's home in Calcutta:

Dear Lord, the Great Healer, I kneel before You,
Since every perfect gift must come from You.
I pray, give skill to my hands, clear vision to my mind, kindness and meekness to my heart.
Give me singleness of purpose, strength to lift up a part of the burden of my

suffering fellow men, and a true
realization of the privilege that is
mine.

Take from my heart all guile and
worldliness,

That with the simple faith of a child, I
may rely on You.

Love is not patronizing and charity isn't about pity, it is about love. Charity and love are the same—with charity you give love, so don't just give money but reach out your hand instead.

L ove has no meaning if it isn't shared. Love has to be put into action. You have to love without expectation, to do something for love itself, not for what you may receive. If you expect something in return, then it isn't love, because true love is loving without conditions and expectations.

The poor are hungry not only for food, they are hungry to be recognized as human beings. They are hungry for dignity and to be treated as we are treated. They are hungry for our love.

EVERY

ACT

OF

LOVE

IS

A

PRAYER

❧

It is not how much you do but how much love you put into the doing and sharing with others that is important. Try not to judge people. If you judge others then you are not giving love.

We must grow in love and to do this we must go on loving and loving and giving and giving until it hurts—the way Jesus did. You must give what will cost you something. Then your gift becomes a sacrifice, which will have value before God. Any sacrifice is useful if it is done out of love.

This giving until it hurts—this sacrifice—is also what I call love in action. Every day I see this love—in children, men, and women.

By becoming poor ourselves, by loving until it hurts, we become capable of loving more deeply, more beautifully, more wholly.

We have to accept suffering with joy, we have to live a life of poverty with cheerful trust and to minister to Jesus in the poorest of the poor with cheerfulness. God loves a cheerful giver. If you are always ready to say Yes to God, you will naturally have a smile for all and be able, with God's blessing, to give until it hurts.

The password of the early Christians was *joy*, so let us still serve the Lord with joy. Joy is love, joy is prayer, joy is strength. God loves a person who gives joyfully, and if you give joyfully you always give more. A joyful heart is the result of a heart burning with love.

Works of love are always works of joy. We don't need to look for happiness: if we have love for others we'll be given it. It is the gift of God.

❧

THE

FRUIT

OF

LOVE

IS

SERVICE

❧

Prayer in action is love, and love in action is service.

We have a sign on the wall of the children's home in Calcutta that reads:

TAKE TIME TO THINK
TAKE TIME TO PRAY
TAKE TIME TO LAUGH

IT IS THE SOURCE OF POWER
IT IS THE GREATEST POWER ON EARTH
IT IS THE MUSIC OF THE SOUL

TAKE TIME TO PLAY
TAKE TIME TO LOVE AND BE LOVED
TAKE TIME TO GIVE

IT IS THE SECRET OF PERPETUAL YOUTH
IT IS GOD'S GIVEN PRIVILEGE
IT IS TOO SHORT A DAY TO BE SELFISH

TAKE TIME TO READ
TAKE TIME TO BE FRIENDLY
TAKE TIME TO WORK

IT IS THE FOUNTAIN OF WISDOM
IT IS THE ROAD TO HAPPINESS
IT IS THE PRICE OF SUCCESS

TAKE TIME TO DO CHARITY
IT IS THE KEY TO HEAVEN.

We are all God's children so it is important to share His gifts. Do not worry about why problems exist in the world—just respond to people's needs.

Works of love are always a means of becoming closer to God.

Our work is constant. The problems of the poor continue, so our work continues. Yet everyone can do something beautiful for God by reaching out to the poor. I see only people filled with God's love, wanting to do works of love. This is the future—this is God's wish for us—to serve through love in action, and to be inspired by the Holy Spirit to act when called.

YOU HAVE COME TO SERVE CHRIST IN THE CRIPPLED, THE SICK AND THE DYING.

WE ARE HAPPY AND THANKFUL THAT YOU HAVE TAKEN THIS OPPORTUNITY TO BE A WITNESS OF GOD'S LOVE IN ACTION.

REMEMBER THAT IT IS CHRIST WHO WORKS THROUGH US—WE ARE MERELY INSTRUMENTS FOR SERVICE.

IT IS NOT HOW MUCH WE DO, BUT HOW MUCH LOVE WE PUT INTO THE DOING.

—from a poster in the Mother House welcoming volunteers

The prayers below are favorites of mine. I give them to people who visit, to guide and help them as they serve others.

☙

Dear Lord, help me to spread thy fragrance everywhere I go.
Flood my soul with Thy spirit and life.
Penetrate and possess my whole being so utterly that all my life may only be a radiance of Thine.
Shine through me, and be so in me that every soul I come in contact with may feel Thy presence in my soul.
Let them look up and see no longer me but only Thee O Lord!

Stay with me, and then I shall begin to shine as Thou shinest; so to shine as to be a light to others.

The light O Lord will be all from Thee; none of it will be mine;

It will be Thou, shining on others through me.

Let me thus praise Thee in the way Thou dost love best, by shining on those around me.

Let me preach Thee without preaching, not by words but by my example, by the catching force, the sympathetic influence of what I do, the evident fullness of the love my heart bears to Thee.

JOHN HENRY CARDINAL NEWMAN

Make us worthy, Lord, to serve our fellow men throughout the world who live and die in poverty and hunger. Give them, through our hands, this day their daily bread; and by our understanding love, give peace and joy.

POPE PAUL VI

But I say again that you don't have to come to India to give love to others—the street you live on can be your Nirmal Hriday.* You can help the poor in your own country.

* The Missionaries of Charity home for the dying in Calcutta.

THE
FRUIT
OF
SERVICE
IS
PEACE

Works of love are always works of peace. Whenever you share love with others, you'll notice the peace that comes to you and to them. When there is peace, there is God—that is how God touches our lives and shows His love for us by pouring peace and joy into our hearts.

> Lead me from death to life,
> From falsehood to truth.
> Lead me from despair to hope,
> From fear to trust.
> Lead me from hate to love,
> From war to peace.
> Let peace fill our hearts,
> Our world our universe
> Peace peace peace.

We have a right to be happy and peaceful. We have been created for this—we are born to be happy—and we can only find true happiness and peace when we are in love with God: there is joy in loving God, great happiness in loving Him.

Many people think that having money makes you happy. I think it must be harder to be happy if you are wealthy because you may find it difficult to see God: you'll have too many other things to think about. However, if God has given you this gift of wealth, then use it for His purpose—help others, help the poor, create jobs, give work to others. Don't waste your wealth. Having food, a home, dignity, freedom, health, and an education are all of God's gifts too, which is why we must help those who are less fortunate than ourselves.

Everything is God's to give and to take away, so share what you've been given, and that includes yourself.

Be happy in the moment, that's enough. Each moment is all we need, not more. Be happy now and if you show through your actions that you love others, including those who are poorer than you, you'll give them happiness, too. It doesn't take much—it can be just giving a smile. The world would be a much better place if everyone smiled more. So smile, be cheerful, be joyous that God loves you.

Finally, I have only one message of peace and that is to love one another as God loves each one of you. Jesus came to give us the good news that God loves us and that He wants us to love one another. And when the time comes to die and go home to God again, we will hear Him say, "Come and possess the Kingdom prepared for you, because I was hungry and you gave me to eat, I was naked and you clothed me, I was sick and you visited me. Whatever you did to the least of my brethren, you did it to me."